JUST GET OVER IT

A Play by
Matthew Garlin

1

Original Concept by
Matthew Garlin & Samantha Davekos

Writing Supervision by
Rebecca Greene

FOR
Megan and Benjamin
and
Natalie

Produced as a Live Zoom Play Reading on September 27th, 2020
Directed by Matthew Garlin

Starring
Damien LaCount as David
Anetta Rauf as Jessica
and
Matthew Garlin Melissa/ Malcolm

AVAILABLE ON THE PODCAST: Everything You Never Needed to Know about
Movies, Music and Theater available on itunes, castbox, spotify, anchor and wherever
you get your podcasts.

INTRODUCTION

So where did this play come from? This play was born out of the most personal and relatable thing: heartbreak and arguing. I haven't had that many relationships but most of them have inspired me to write this play. So I have recently come to terms with a lot of my past and saying I'm sorry for a lot of things I have done in the past and so part of that is to get over any heartbreak or hang ups I still have from past relationships. Sometimes they stay with you for a while but I am happy to say that things happened the way they were supposed to happen and things are very great with me now considering how lucky I am to have the family I have.

The idea of putting these characters in a very unlikely and not realistic situation made sense to me because I have always been interested in writing about a broken up couple trying to put the pieces together either to get back together again or to just figure out where they went wrong. Also as I have mentioned in my other books, I love listening to people arguing and so any chance to have people argue in one room is like the best thing for me as a playwright.

As I stated before, prior relationships have inspired much of this play. I'm not saying I am David but there are some personal moments and situations in this play. This is a rather personal play but I wrote these characters as far away from my own feelings and characteristics so that people who play David or even Jessica, don't think I am either of the characters. I will say that some of what David says about his insecurities or him thinking he's not a good person are things that I have felt before. I have done some terrible things to women in the past in relationships. I haven't beaten them or anything like that, but I've been manipulative and controlling and for that I apologize. I have also acted selfishly in a lot of circumstances and I do apologize for that. I am thankfully friends with a few of them and I am very grateful that there can be a second life and that we don't have to dwell on the past.

Anyway, I hope people can relate to this play and I hope people like this play.

Sincerely,

Matthew Garlin

Matthew Garlin
Playwright

CHARACTERS
David
Jessica

Melissa
Malcolm

ACT ONE

Scene opens with David in the living area (sitting area). He's sitting on a couch with a coffee table to the side of him. There are two armchairs on either side of the couch with a table on the left and a TV stand with a 42-inch flat screen on it. Through the back way is a door that is propped open showing a bathroom with a toilet and shower. David is on the phone pacing.

DAVID

Hello? Hello? Is this the front desk? (Pause) Awesome, can I get an update? (Pause) An update on the situation going on right now? (Pause) Who am I? I'm the guy asking you for an update on the situation going on right now. (Pause) I mean with the storm. (Pause) Yes, I understand you don't work the weather channel but…(Pause) Look, I just want to know how long we are going to be stuck in this hotel for the night because…I, out of the kindness of my heart, am sharing a room with a woman I dated for 4 years and well…things aren't going well. (Pause) No, I can speak freely because she's down getting food which by the way, why is there no room service right now? (Pause) yes I understand that there's a storm going on, did I not just ask for an update to the storm like 3 seconds ago? (Pause) This is a 5 star hotel right? (Pause) Well, you are going to lose one star from the review I will give you on yelp for the treatment I have felt from you! You have not been professional and efficient at all. (Pause) Yes, I understand you are the only hotel open right now but that doesn't excuse unprofessionalism. (Pause) Yes, I will do that to myself after I do it to your mother! (hangs up). Overpaid doorknob….

David sits in the armchair. A knock comes to the door. He gets up and goes to the door.

DAVID

Who is it?

JESSICA (OS)
It's me...

DAVID
Who's me?

JESSICA (OS)
You're mother, open the door!

DAVID
How do I know it's you? You could be a robber using a fake voice to find
your way in here and then rob me blind and have your way with me.

JESSICA (OS)
Open the door, you ridiculous crouton!

DAVID
What's the secret password?

JESSICA (OS)
Let me in!

DAVID
No, that's not it.

JESSICA (OS)
You want to eat, let me in!

DAVID
Is that my only choice?

JESSICA (OS)
David...

DAVID
Why do you not have a key to the room if this is your room, huh? There
I run rings around you logically.

All of a sudden, a click comes to the door as it opens showing Jessica
standing there balancing a box of food and a key card in her hands.

JESSICA
You really could have been nicer and let me in...

DAVID
You could have been nicer and asked nicer

Jessica hands David the box of food.

JESSICA
You own me 15 bucks

DAVID
I only wanted a sandwich

JESSICA
And a coke?

DAVID
Yes

JESSICA
A sandwich and a coke?

DAVID
Yes

JESSICA
You wanted a sandwich and a coke.

DAVID
Yes

JESSICA
Okay, it cost 15 bucks

DAVID
No, see it can't cost 15 bucks, you know why?

JESSICA
Why?

DAVID
Because I only wanted a sandwich and a coke

JESSICA
A sandwich and a coke cost 15 bucks

DAVID
A sandwich and a coke for 15 bucks, what is this, Fenway Park?!

Jessica
Yes, it is, you know why?

DAVID
Why?

JESSICA
Because you owe me 15 bucks for your sandwich and coke!

DAVID
Ugh, but...(Thinking) but I saved your life!

JESSICA
Oh please.

DAVID
No, I saved your life!

JESSICA
You saved my life?

DAVID
Yes!

JESSICA
You saved shit!

DAVID
That transformer was going to fall on you, and I grabbed you and pulled
you out of the way of it!

JESSICA (realizing something)
You were the one who pulled me out of the way as a transformer was
about the land on me?

DAVID
Yes!

JESSICA (more loving)

You did that?

DAVID
Yes!

JESSICA
You dislocated my shoulder.

DAVID
Okay…

JESSICA
No wonder it's been killing me ever since.

DAVID
I still saved your life!

JESSICA
No, you didn't

DAVID
Yes, I did, and you know why?

JESSICA
No why?

DAVID
Because I pulled you out of the way of that transformer.

JESSICA
David, that transformer was 50-60 yards away from me and I know that
because I was at the front door of the hotel and if I had been crushed
by that transformer 50-60 yards away, I would have still been alive

since the transformer which was 50-60 yards away was only 50-60 years away! We're not talking the leaning tower of electricity or the Eiffel tower of transformers. So, no you didn't save my life, but I thank you for letting me share the hotel room and in gratitude, I'm on going to charge you 14 bucks for the sandwich and coke, what do you say to that?

DAVID
Maybe I shouldn't have saved your life.

JESSICA
You didn't save my life!

DAVID
Yes, it did!

JESSICA
I have 5 eyewitnesses who say no! want to know how I know that?

DAVID
Okay, how?

JESSICA
Cause there were five people standing next you who if they thought I was in danger would have been faster than the 30 seconds you waited to grab me from the falling transformer.

DAVID
You timed me?!

JESSICA
Didn't have to

DAVID
You timed me?

JESSICA
I really didn't have to?

DAVID
Why?

JESSICA
Because I held my breath?!

DAVID
Ugh

JESSICA
Come on, I know you

DAVID
You know me?

JESSICA
Yes!

DAVID
You know shit!

JESSICA
I know you try to figure things out before acting. I know that you pride yourself in protecting me and I know that you are going to give me the 15 dollars for the sandwich and coke.

DAVID

14...

JESSICA
Ha! I knew I'd get you!

DAVID
Ugh!

David reaches into his pocket and gives Jessica 14 bucks.

DAVID
Gold-digger

JESSICA
Honey, I'm not married to you and I have a job

DAVID
So?

JESSICA
So just eat your sandwich.

DAVID
If it cost anymore, I'd be sending it off to college and hoping it
graduates as summa cum laude

JESSICA
I don't know how you eat that stuff

DAVID
What stuff?

JESSICA

That stuff.

DAVID
Bread?

JESSICA
No...

DAVID
Cheese?

JESSICA
No...

DAVID
Mayonnaise?

JESSICA
No! meat...

DAVID
Oh no, not this again

JESSICA
Do you know how many animals were killed for you to have the
sandwich?

DAVID
You know how many trees you killed for you know…. Paper!

JESSICA
Good come back, you write that one yourself.

DAVID
I'm not as fast as you when it comes to…you know…umm…you know…

JESSICA
Come backs?

DAVID
Don't help me, I would have thought of it!

JESSICA
Does it bother you that you're eating an animal?

DAVID
Does it bother you that your hair is wet?

JESSICA
No, does it bother you?

DAVID
A little bit.

JESSICA
Well build a bridge and get over it.

DAVID
Where the hell is this going?

JESSICA
Does it bother you that you are eating animals? Animals who do nothing but frolic…

DAVID
Frolic?

JESSICA
Frolic!

DAVID
I got news for you, animals don't frolic, they...umm they...

JESSICA
I'll be done with my dinner by the time you think up something,

DAVID
They eat grass and poop

JESSICA
So, you're an animal

DAVID
Ha...ha, and some animals eat other animals

JESSICA
To survive

DAVID
Yes, but they forage on themselves so doesn't that bother you?

JESSICA
No but does it both you?

DAVID
No! it doesn't because ham tastes delicious, turkey is amazing and roast
beef is like my crack! And I have no qualms about any of that because I
am an addict and I need my fix!

JESSICA
You're ridiculous

DAVID
How can you only eat vegetables?

JESSICA
How?

DAVID
Yes how? How do you eat vegetables?

JESSICA
Usually with a fork but sometimes with my hands.

DAVID
That's not what I mean!

JESSICA
I eat it knowing I haven't killed anything

DAVID
I got news for you; veggies are things!

JESSICA
Things?

DAVID
They are living breathing things!

JESSICA
What are you talking about?

DAVID
You know what I mean!

JESSICA
I really don't.

DAVID
Veggies live and breathe and get nutrients from the sun so in fact they
are living breathing things so are you saying that they are lower of the
chain of food as you know other things.

JESSICA
Do you hear yourself right now?

DAVID
I go in and out.

JESSICA
Do you want me to starve?

DAVID
Well you could lose some weight...

JESSICA
Excuse me?!

DAVID
Who said that?

JESSICA
I could lose some weight?

DAVID

Did I say that?

JESSICA
Well what about you?

DAVID
What about me?

JESSICA
Any more weight and you could be a sumo wrestler, you fat ass!

DAVID
I'm not feeling the love tonight, Jess.

JESSICA
Oh, you'll feel the love tonight when I knee you in the balls!

DAVID
I saved you your life!

JESSICA
From a 10ft transformer 50-60 yards away from me?!

DAVID
I saved your life! I told you to stay close to me.

JESSICA
I wanted to see how bad it was raining.

DAVID
You left me!

(Pause)

JESSICA
What?

DAVID
I mean...you left my side

JESSICA
Did you say, I left you?

DAVID
No...

JESSICA
Don't

DAVID
What?

JESSICA
Don't

DAVID
I just did

JESSICA
Don't!

DAVID
I did!

JESSICA
You better not

DAVID
Yes, I just did

JESSICA
We are not going to talk about that at all tonight or ever again?!

DAVID
Oh, we're not?

JESSICA
No, we are going to sit here and eat our murdered meals in silence

They both sit down and begin to eat their dinners as they both look around awkwardly.

JESSICA
But I was right

DAVID
Christ, you couldn't resist

JESSICA
What?

DAVID
You couldn't have just left it alone.

JESSICA
You wanted to talk about it

DAVID
I did?

JESSICA
You brought it up?

DAVID
I was kidding

JESSICA
And yet here we are, we are now going to talk about that

DAVID
No, not that, let's not talk about that

JESSICA
Oh yes that!

DAVID
Let's talk about the carcasses of animals more

JESSICA
David?!

DAVID
You really want to talk about this?

JESSICA
Yes!

DAVID
Fine! I never knew how to cook!

JESSICA
Why do you lie?

DAVID
You have no evidence that I have lied about anything else?

JESSICA
Oh honey, the things I know...

DAVID
But I tried.

JESSICA
How many fires did we have in our kitchen?

DAVID
It wasn't THAT bad!

JESSICA
Our landlord forbad you to using the stove!

DAVID
That is an exaggeration!

JESSICA
You're right...he also forbad you using the microwave!

DAVID
Jessica...

JESSICA
I mean, I understand not knowing the correct temperature for baking
bread, but how does someone burn jello!!!

DAVID

You are loving this, aren't you?

JESSICA
I'm just saying that that $14 sandwich might be your only meal if we
lose power.

DAVID
I could whip us up something in the kitchen!

JESSICA
David, you just saw a transformer collapse and fire outside the hotel,
now do you really want to see flames inside of this room!

DAVID
Well I haven't turned on my charm yet.

JESSICA
Oh honey, I am immune to your charm.

DAVID
Really? I don't know about that!

JESSICA
Please, just eat your dinner and know that I was right, and you were
wrong.

DAVID
It wasn't a matter of being right or wrong, it was a matter that I tried
and failed but nevertheless I tried.

JESSICA
I grant you one point. Here is a dollar back, your sandwich only cost $13
bucks. While you're at it, buy a clue.

DAVID
You know I keep this charm up, I'll get my money back.

JESSICA
Honey don't even try. You aren't as charming as you think you are.

DAVID
You're right...some people didn't think so.

JESSICA
Yes indeed...wait what?

DAVID
What?

JESSICA
What does that mean?

DAVID
I don't know.

JESSICA
Yes, you do, you fool! Were you trying to say something about something?

DAVID
Well I tried to charm your friends and I never really got anywhere.

JESSICA
Well they did think you were hitting on them and in retrospect, I can see their point.

DAVID
I was trying to be nice to them since they were YOUR friends, you could
have tried with mine.

JESSICA
All your friends wanted to talk about was football…

DAVID
Okay and?

JESSICA
I hate football! Now baseball, I could get into but the minute we all got
together, "oh Smith went way down and caught it on the 45 but he
couldn't find his way to Boston, nevermind, the endzone for a Hail
Mary touchdown".

DAVID
Well he is a mite rusty.

JESSICA
None of that makes sense to me.

DAVID
Well…

JESSICA
And don't explain it to me.

DAVID
Why?

JESSICA

Because like almost every other woman out there, when a man mansplains something, it's just a turn off.

DAVID
Ah! So, you were turned on…

JESSICA
Oh my god! Spare me!

DAVID
Why don't you just admit the truth, you never liked my friends and your friends labeled me a womanizer!

JESSICA
I liked your friends fine, it was Ralph, I couldn't stand.

DAVID
Ralph was fine.

JESSICA
He's an alcoholic.

DAVID
No, he's not, he just doesn't know when to stop drinking.

JESSICA
OH! He doesn't know when to stop, huh?

DAVID
No…

JESSICA
Oh, I see, you want to know something…

DAVID
What?

JESSICA
THAT'S WHAT AN ALCOHOLIC IS!!!!!!!

DAVID
I wouldn't know but you have the same experience.

JESSICA
What's that supposed to me?

DAVID
I never liked your mother?!

JESSICA
What?

DAVID
I never liked your mother; she was a pain in the ass

JESSICA
Really?

DAVID
Yes.... oh, you never knew that?

JESSICA
No

DAVID

Well, there it is. That woman would know the definition of an alcoholic!
She's never met a wine she didn't like or finish!

(Pause)

JESSICA
You never liked my mother?

DAVID
Did I say that?

JESSICA
Just now!

DAVID
I've moved on to other things in my head.

JESSICA
Why didn't you like my mom?!

DAVID
Who? That lovely lady?

JESSICA
David?!

DAVID
I got news for you; it was mutual!!

JESSICA
She loved you!

DAVID

I asked her if I could visit her on one of my company trips. And For my birthday, she gave me a map of Texas!

JESSICA
So?

DAVID
She lives in Alaska?!

JESSICA
I can see how that can be confusing

DAVID
Jess!

JESSICA
She is a lovely woman and she treated you with respect

DAVID
She called me fat ass!

JESSICA
Well you were a little heavy...

DAVID
I am not responsible for what I say about a woman who spent her days sticking bobby pins into a homemade voodoo doll of me

JESSICA
Now you are just being ridiculous

DAVID
Am I?

JESSICA
How do you know this stuff, did you spy on her?

DAVID
Jessica, she put it on Facebook.

JESSICA
She did?

DAVID
She has a page that says, the schmuck my daughter is settling for!

JESSICA
What? She put a status change of stabbing a voodoo doll?

DAVID
Not exactly!

JESSICA
You are overreacting.

DAVID
You are dramatically underreacting

JESSICA
She changed her status to stabbing a voodoo doll? I don't believe that.

DAVID
She put up pictures!

JESSICA
What?

DAVID
She put up pictures saying "David, I'm going to get you"

JESSICA
I can't help you there.

DAVID
you can't help me anywhere! And I wasn't asking for help

JESSICA
Well good

DAVID
Good

JESSICA
Okay

DAVID
Okay!

JESSICA
Fine!

DAVID
Fine!

JESSICA
David!

DAVID
What?

JESSICA
Why are we yelling?!

DAVID
I don't know... (stopping himself from yelling) I don't know...we always
seemed to yell.

JESSICA
Really?

DAVID
I guess

JESSICA
Well...when we first met...

DAVID
Oh god!

JESSICA
When we first met...

DAVID
Oh God!

JESSICA
When we first met...

DAVID
Jesus!!

JESSICA

Before you get to the holy spirit, when we first met, we argued all night.

DAVID
Don't remind me…

JESSICA
We spent the entire night arguing

DAVID
You don't have to tell me I was there

JESSICA
What did we argue about?

DAVID
The capitalistic view of modernization in blah blah blah. It was one of those conversations you wish you never started

JESSICA
I was stating that capitalism of America is a good and bad thing and how the democrats and republicans are the extremes of a very pointed circle.

DAVID
And all I wanted was bean dip

JESSICA
You were interested

DAVID
You were standing in front of the bead dip!

JESSICA
You couldn't take your eyes off

DAVID
Bean dip!!

JESSICA
So that's why you started to talk to me? Because of some crummy ass
bean dip?

DAVID
You were an attractive girl standing in front of the bead dip, I am not a
moron.

JESSICA
You debated with me all night

DAVID
I have a talent of defending points and not really believing a thing that I
say.

JESSICA
You didn't believe anything you were saying, but you were sounding
convincing!

DAVID
I really am quite something!

JESSICA
So, you were lying?

DAVID
Devil's advocate is a great stance on any argument

JESSICA
You were lying?!

DAVID
Yea basically

JESSICA
Liar!

DAVID
Jessica...

JESSICA
We argued until 3. And you just stood there.

DAVID
Again, you are hot and I'm not a moron.

JESSICA
Jesus you probably don't remember anything else about that night.

DAVID
We ended up on a college soccer field, you were carrying your shoes in your left hand. You had that blue turquoise dress on looking like you should have been in a Disney parade. You were saying things I knew you were passionate about so that's why I stayed.

JESSICA
You stayed because you thought you were going to get laid. Your talent is failing you, sweetheart.

DAVID

But I stayed.

JESSICA
You did and so did I!

DAVID
Yes, you did too, why did you stay?

JESSICA
I'm sorry?

DAVID
I was making mild points to your passionate side of the argument.
Clearly, I was not smart enough to say anything that toppled your
argument and I was in a lower league than yourself, why did you stay?

JESSICA
You were cute and I thought I was getting laid.

DAVID
Hold the phone...Wait a minute, I spent that whole time listening to you
and we didn't even have sex!!!

JESSICA
No, we didn't

DAVID
But we could have?

JESSICA
I wasn't wearing any underwear

DAVID

NOW SHE TELLS ME!!

JESSICA
I thought you stayed because you liked what I was saying?

DAVID
I stayed because I wanted to get laid; I didn't even understand what
you were saying.

JESSICA
Oh well...

DAVID
Do you know how cold of a shower I had to take?

JESSICA
Not my fault

DAVID
It's 100% your fault!

JESSICA
Eat your sandwich

DAVID
No!

JESSICA
David!

DAVID
What?

JESSICA
Eat your sandwich!

DAVID
Why?

JESSICA
Because it's food and it was a very expensive sandwich

DAVID
Oh yes let's change the subject, shall we?

JESSICA
and you should eat it before we…

Light go out

JESSICA
Lose power

DAVID
I can't find my sandwich

JESSICA
Told you.

DAVID
Where's my 9-dollar sandwich?

JESSICA
13 dollars, Jesus?!

End of Act one

ACT TWO

Lights come up as David enters with Jessica sitting on a couch with her head in her hands.

DAVID

It has been fixed! I am the master! The master of electricity! Bow down before me! I summon fire from the sky!!

JESSICA

Can you be any more of an idiot?

DAVID

You are just jealous because you cannot summon fire from the sky?!

JESSICA

Summon fire from the sky? Who are you Zeus?

DAVID

No, I am the Master of Electricity?! I am the Sorcerer of Fuses! The...

JESSICA

You are the master of being an idiot?!

DAVID

Do you seem me reveling?!

JESSICA
What?

DAVID
Reveling?! I am reveling it all

JESSICA
I can hear it mostly

DAVID
I have always been very handy

JESSICA
In what century?

DAVID
I fixed your father's TV

JESSICA
You also broke my mom's table; how do you fix a TV one minute and
the next break the table it's placed upon? Huh? Answer me that Mr.
Master of Electricity? Summon that answer from the sky?!

DAVID
Hey something electronic was fixed...

JESSICA
And something made out of wood was broken?!

DAVID
Hey...hey...hey

JESSICA
You tried to fix it the entire time. And that, ladies and gentlemen, was my parents' introduction to my boyfriend. The man who can fix a TV but destroy a table in one bound without having eaten anything.

DAVID
I was trying to be seen as...umm

JESSICA
Useful? Are you an idiot?

DAVID
Yes useful.

JESSICA
Why? Why did you go through that torture? You know what happened I ended up falling asleep with my parents at the dinner table waiting for you! Why?

DAVID
Because?! I was trying to impress you.

JESSICA
I'm sorry

DAVID
I was trying to impress you

JESSICA
You were?

DAVID
Yes.

JESSICA
How pathetic

DAVID
Excuse me?

JESSICA
You pretended to know internal hardware and electronics to try to
impress me?

DAVID (More defensive)
Maybe.

JESSICA
So, every time you tried to fix something, you pretended to know what
you were doing?

DAVID
Pretty much.

JESSICA
Didn't you try to fix my sister's pipes?

DAVID
Yea...

JESSICA
What happened?

DAVID
Let's not talk about it.

JESSICA
Why?

DAVID
Didn't end well

JESSICA
Why didn't it end well?

DAVID
Don't worry about it

JESSICA
What did you do?

DAVID
Nothing...

JESSICA
What did you do?!

DAVID
I may have...may have...and remember this was coming from a place of
love

JESSICA
Tell me

DAVID
I may have and here is where I should get points.

JESSICA
What?

DAVID
I may have flooded her basement

JESSICA
What?

DAVID
I may have flooded her basement

JESSICA
Are you kidding me?

DAVID
In retrospect, I probably should have called a plumber

JESSICA
You think?

DAVID
I'm just saying

JESSICA
You flooded...my sister's...basement...why didn't I hear about this before?

DAVID
She was sworn to secrecy

JESSICA
Why didn't I hear about this before?

DAVID

I am very crafty

JESSICA
DAVID?!

DAVID
I paid her for her discretion, are you a moron?

JESSICA
What?

DAVID
I gave her money to fix it correctly. That why I didn't take you out for
our anniversary and why she never called the house and sent you
obscene amount of text messages

JESSICA
OOO I see

DAVID
I mean I did the right thing.

JESSICA
You flooded my sister's basement, paid her off and then didn't tell me
about it? That's what you did?

DAVID
Yes...

JESSICA
Well that makes sense now. I understand

Jessica starts to laugh and David, who sees she's not going to kill him, slowly starts to laugh too.

JESSICA
I'm going to drown you in the bathtub and then make a sandwich and watch the new episode of the Bachelor!!

DAVID
Jessica…

JESSICA
How could you have done this to me and kept it from me this long

DAVID
Was it that long?

JESSICA
Excuse me?!

DAVID
I was being sincere

JESSICA
You were being an ass

DAVID
An ass, an ass, I'm an ass, I'm an ass!

JESSICA
Keep telling yourself until you believe it!

DAVID

To impress you…I was… am an ass because I was trying to impress you!
Because I wanted to help out your family member? That makes me an
ass

JESSICA
No

DAVID
good

JESSICA
It makes you a well-meaning ass!

DAVID
It's not like you didn't do anything to try to impress me.

JESSICA
I'm sorry was I supposed to impress you

DAVID
No but…

JESSICA
…you have no proof I tried to impress you

DAVID
You know what? You're right.

(PAUSE)

JESSICA
Do you?

DAVID
Hmm?

JESSICA
Do you?

DAVID
Do I what?

JESSICA
Do you have proof that I tried to impress you?

DAVID
No...nope, no fact, no nothing.

JESSICA
David?!

DAVID
Hmm?

JESSICA
David! What did my sister tell you?

DAVID
What?

JESSICA
What did my sister tell you?

DAVID
Nothing

JESSICA
David?!

DAVID
Nothing, oh by the way how's that guitar practice going?

JESSICA
Excuse me?

DAVID
Guitar practice?

JESSICA
What do you mean?

DAVID
How long have you been playing again?

JESSICA
Umm, since I was in 5th grade.

DAVID
That's what I thought you said.

JESSICA
What do you think you know?

DAVID
Apparently, nothing

JESSICA
David, I will beat you with a potato gun

DAVID
You learned a week after we met?!

JESSICA
What...I...what?

DAVID
When we met, it was at that bar during open mic night.

JESSICA
Right...

DAVID
We argued all night afterwards

JESSICA
Right...

DAVID
And I said to one of your friends that a sexy thing indeed is a woman
with a guitar and some cowboy boots.

JESSICA
Okay...

DAVID
And that I would enjoy in a feminist way to have a girl serenade me
with a guitar and some cowboy boots.

JESSICA
Where is this going?

DAVID

You learned how to play the guitar a week after we met!

JESSICA
I did not!

DAVID
Jessica...

JESSICA
What?

DAVID
I know!

JESSICA
What?

DAVID
You had your sister buy the guitar so it wouldn't be traced back to you and you taught yourself then you went to Marshall's and bought brown Taylor Swift cowboy boots. You made it look like you kept forgetting your guitar until 6 months later and you walk out of the bedroom with nothing but a guitar and some cowboy boots and played four of the easiest songs in the world to try to impress me. That, Mrs. Lincoln, is how you did that!

JESSICA
They weren't that easy...

DAVID
Colonel Mustard in the library with the wrench, motherfucker?!

JESSICA

Okay calm down, how did you...

DAVID
She Told Me?! I'm not Sherlock...umm Sherlock...

JESSICA
Holmes...

DAVID
I know his name! Yeah, I'm not Sherlock Holmes, I'm not Columbo asking one last question. I'm not the thin man!

JESSICA
That's for sure...

DAVID
She told me only to show you did like me once. And to tell me that she thought it was weird that you had her buy it for you which you haven't paid her back for by the way.

JESSICA
Well...I...I

DAVID
You didn't want it traced back to you, what are you, Professor Moriarity?

JESSICA
Well I...

DAVID
Why couldn't you just admit you were trying to impress me?

JESSICA
Well…

DAVID
Why are you so proud? Did your mother inundate you so well that a woman stand on her own two feed and blah, blah, blah that you decided that romance meant arguing with a man instead of holding hands in public?

JESSICA
Well why didn't you tell me about the flooding with my sister? You really pretended to know about indoor plumbing? Why didn't you just say, I don't know how to do this, get someone who can. Why are you so proud and stubborn?

DAVID
That's different.

JESSICA
I don't see how, you claim I am proud and too proud to admit I'm wrong or that I was trying to impress you, well how about a man who openly checked out 2 women on our first year anniversary and pretended to cough, to say nothing of the fact that your idea of complimenting me was telling me my teeth were nice?

DAVID
They were…

JESSICA
I learned something I never learned before. I actually practiced and practiced, you just pretended, that's the difference, Huckleberry. And again…you are an ass…

(Pause)

DAVID
I'm surprised we got to a year.

JESSICA
What do you mean?

DAVID
Well it sounds like it was such a horrible time.

JESSICA
I didn't say that.

DAVID
And I'm such an ass

JESSICA
I never said that...much

DAVID
You didn't...you just call me an ass a bunch of times in a row!

JESSICA
David...

DAVID
The first date was great, okay, like a high on the realm of awesomeness but until we hit date five, they kept getting constantly worst. Like every date, kept getting worst and worst.

JESSICA

They weren't that...okay yes, that first date did put a high expectation
for the rest of them.

DAVID
It was a lot of fun!

JESSICA
Are you kidding? The museum of fine arts is always a trip.

DAVID
Well I worked my magic

JESSICA
What magic?

DAVID
You remember the exhibit?

JESSICA
Yeah, the art of Asia

DAVID
Yeah?

JESSICA
What?

DAVID
You love Asia.

JESSICA
Are you kidding? It's a place I have always wished to go.

DAVID
You know how I was surprised that we timed going there during that exhibit?

JESSICA
Yea but so what they have...(inhales) You Knew!!

DAVID
Well...like a magician I don't like to explain my tricks to a...

JESSICA
You fucking knew?!

DAVID
What? I didn't even read the papers in those days.

JESSICA
You motherfucker?!

DAVID
Temper...

JESSICA
I can't believe you...

DAVID
Jess...

JESSICA
I can't believe...

DAVID
Did you have fun?

JESSICA
What?

DAVID
Did you have fun?

JESSICA
Well...

DAVID
Did you?

JESSICA
That's not the point.

DAVID
Well let's make it the point. Let's make it the point that you actually had fun. Let's actually take that into consideration not just that you are mad and that somewhere in this godforsaken world I wronged you, but let's throw that on the table that you had fun. Fun was had and you had it!

JESSICA
Okay fine, yes, I had fun!

DAVID
Fine!

(PAUSE)

JESSICA
So, what's your point?

DAVID
My point is…. umm…aha ha! You had fun! Ladies and gentlemen of the
court, she had fun…

JESSICA
Yes…

DAVID
You had fun

JESSICA
Yes!

DAVID
She had fun, Fun was had, and she had it. There was something fun
going on and it was Jessica who was experiencing it.

Jessica just glares at David.

DAVID
And how much fun?

JESSICA
Don't push it

DAVID
She had tons of fun!!

JESSICA
Yes, I had fun, yes you won major points with the museum trip and
then dinner later. Yes, you did everything you were supposed to do, but

at what point did you think you could be a complete douchebag and
snowball all of that?

DAVID
What did I do to you? Did I kill you dog? Maim your sister? Mutilate
your mother?

JESSICA
Why did it take you 4 months to admit you loved me?

DAVID
That's what this is about?

JESSICA
Part of it, we'll get to the rest later, right now, we are here. Why did It
take you four months to admit you loved me?

DAVID
I am a cautious person.

JESSICA
Seriously?!

DAVID
Jess...

JESSICA
If you were in love with you, why wasn't I the first person you told, why
did you tell Perry first?

DAVID
Listen to me...

JESSICA
I don't understand for the life of me why you need probing to admit
your feelings

DAVID
Listen to me now

JESSICA
I have been listening and all I hear is smoke-filled candy-ass bullshit.
Why didn't you have the balls to tell me how you felt, why did your
friend tell me how you felt in a text?!

DAVID
Because I was scared

(PAUSE)

JESSICA
What?

DAVID
I was scared.

JESSICA
Why?

DAVID
Jess, do you have any clue about anything?

JESSICA
Enlighten me please, I realize my boyfriend of 4 years has no balls.

DAVID

You don't get it at all. Where on your list of priority does trust come into play? Is it before or after being a bitch? Trust is like high on the list before breathing is even a thought, I believe in trust!

JESSICA
Okay, so you have no balls, but you believe in trust?

DAVID
No, I am a person who wants to make sure the girl won't flee the minute the walls come down.

JESSICA
Dav…

DAVID
Jessica! Look at me, look at me, there is no way in the hell a girl like you chooses a guy like me over every other guy out there. The fact that you said yes to dinner the first time surprised the hell out of me. Believe it or not, I didn't trust my luck. Nor did I actually believe you'd say, Yes. Yes, it took me four months to admit I loved you, yes I couldn't even tell you and so I told my best friend Perry, who like the took he is, texted you an hour after he and I hung out, but you know wanna know something? I knew I loved you on our fourth date. That's the truth and I trusted you on our second date. I fell in love with you the minute I saw you, but that's not normal and I was trying to be normal.

JESSICA
You think not telling me when you fell in love with me was not normal?

DAVID
Not the moment I met you.

JESSICA

I wouldn't have been scared and I don't understand why you were
surprised; you were and are still cute.

DAVID
But not normal.

JESSICA
Well no one is normal, that's the beauty of it. I do have one question
though.

DAVID
Yes?

JESSICA
You fell in love with me on our fourth date…

DAVID
Yes

JESSICA
What was wrong with our first three?

David is speechless and then Jessica starts to laugh.

JESSICA
I'm kidding.

(Pause)

JESSICA
It took you until the fourth date to fall in love with me?

DAVID

Jessica!

JESSICA
You fell in love with me on our fourth date?

DAVID
Yeah...

JESSICA
David...we were in jail!

DAVID
Yeah, so?

JESSICA
And That was a horrible experience. All I wanted to do is go dancing.

DAVID
Oh, you mean the Joker's Club?

JESSICA
Yeah, all I wanted was a nice fun night at the club and dance.

DAVID
Instead I got a chair to the head.

JESSICA
When?

DAVID
Right before the riot.

JESSICA

The dude hit you in the head with a chair?

DAVID
I felt like I was in the WWF.

They laugh

DAVID
And do you remember what you said when we were in jail?

JESSICA
No…

DAVID
You said "I'm not drunk, I don't have a black eye, and I'm not a prostitute but I'm in jail. Gotta love America".

Jessica laughs

DAVID
The fact that everything that could go wrong did, but that you were still with a sense of humor, it showed me who you were. I fell in love that instant.

JESSICA
But you waited…

DAVID
I was afraid you'd leave. So yes, I have no balls, but I believe in trust.

(Pause)

JESSICA

You know when I fell in love with you?

DAVID
No

JESSICA
Remember our 5th date?

DAVID
The open mic night?

JESSICA
Yea…

DAVID
When I actually got up there and sang?

JESSICA
Solo act, no one next to you

DAVID
Yea

JESSICA
You were so cute Thinking you could sing

DAVID
I can sing

JESSICA
That's cute

DAVID

No! I can sing!

JESSICA
Less cute now.

DAVID
I took singing lessons

JESSICA
On purpose?

DAVID
Three years I took singing lessons, it took 3 years for me to learn how to
sing

JESSICA
Wow three wasted years huh?

DAVID
Hey…

JESSICA
And you were yelling at me about the price of sandwich and you paid
for singing lessons?!

(Pause)

JESSICA
You didn't pay for singing lessons?

(Pause)

JESSICA

You got free singing lessons for three years?

DAVID
My grandma taught me...

JESSICA
Nana Darlene?

DAVID
Yes! Nana Darlene! She gave me singing lessons.

JESSICA
Nana Darlene gave you singing lessons...

DAVID
Yes!

JESSICA
David?

DAVID
Yes?

JESSICA
The woman is deaf?!

DAVID
No, she isn't

JESSICA
Physically deaf and tone-deaf

DAVID

No, she isn't?!

JESSICA
She heard Pavarotti sing and thought he was too sharp

DAVID
Well...maybe he was

JESSICA
He's an accomplished opera singer, the man runs rings around Justin
Bieber and all three of the Jonas Brothers.

DAVID
What's your point?

JESSICA
She gave you singing lessons and so you think you are a good singer?

DAVID
I am!

JESSICA
David, just because a person is taught to sing doesn't mean they should
look at Broadway.

DAVID
Yes, it does

JESSICA
That's like a guy who is taught how to hold a hammer thinking he can
build a whole fucking house.

DAVID

Well whatever, I can sing and maybe that guy can build a house, if only someone encouraged him.

JESSICA
I do encourage you when the situation calls for encouraging.

DAVID
You always shoot my ideas down, my great ideas.

JESSICA
David, you wanted to go an astronaut once

DAVID
Yes?

JESSICA
Do you realize how long it takes to train for something like that?

DAVID
All I needed was google.

JESSICA
All you needed was a clue!!

DAVID
There you go bringing me down.

JESSICA
Listen, I was a good girlfriend, I treated you nice and wonderful and yea, maybe I didn't go for all of your crazy ideas, but I was still there for you, shaking my head but there for you.

DAVID

And it all began on that night at the open mic night when I sang my heart out to you.

JESSICA
Off key yes

DAVID
Fine whatever

JESSICA
Well I thought you were cute, and I fell for you.

DAVID
I bet you thought I was cute at our 2-year anniversary.

JESSICA
Hold on, I have to tell you something about our first year.

DAVID
What is that?

JESSICA
It was fun! I loved getting to know you, getting to know your friends, that was what was fun.

DAVID
My family?

JESSICA
Getting to know your family as well.

DAVID
If only our families could cohabitate

JESSICA
Our families got along fine.

DAVID
Your father hated me, and your mother thought I was one of the Dobie Brothers.

JESSICA
Well you're mother thought I was too athletic, and your father thought I was too fat.

DAVID
He did not!

JESSICA
He called me chubby?!

DAVID
And what did you call him?

JESSICA
Baldy!

DAVID
Was that nice?

JESSICA
Nicer than calling someone chubby?!

DAVID
Your cousins found me absolutely repulsive

JESSICA
Wait? My cousins?

DAVID
Harold and Jen?

JESSICA
Harold and Jen?

DAVID
Yes, Harold and Jen...

JESSICA
Harold and Jen thought you were repulsive?

DAVID
Yes?!

JESSICA
Do you mean Heidi and James?

DAVID
What?

JESSICA
Harold and Jen have been dead for 10 years, Heidi and James liked you fine, you were being sarcastic with them when they were talking about having their baby.

DAVID
They kept saying we are having a baby, we are pregnant

JESSICA

So?

DAVID
HE is not pregnant. She is pregnant, he just gets 2 months a paid time
off because of it.

JESSICA
They were excited

DAVID
They were also being stupid?!

JESSICA
Well at least, their kids don't steal things

DAVID
What you mean?

JESSICA
I mean your cousin Phil, Phillip. He stole my pens all the time.

DAVID
He wanted to be a writer.

JESSICA
He was stabbing me in the leg with them.

DAVID
He was trying to be funny.

JESSICA
I bled twice.

DAVID
He was just being cute.

JESSICA
Like you were?

DAVID
Right!

JESSICA
And how were you cute during our 2nd year?

DAVID
Who gave you a romantic carriage ride in the park?

JESSICA
The carriage ride in the park?

DAVID
Yes, the carriage ride in the park

JESSICA
You mean the one we witnessed a mugging and had to call the cops and then explain what we saw? That carriage ride in the park?

DAVID
I may be remembering it different

JESSICA
You think?

DAVID
It was still romantic

JESSICA
It was very romantic

DAVID
See?

JESSICA
Apart from the mugging in the park and the cops, it was very romantic.

DAVID
See I did some cute things from time to time.

JESSICA
Yes, like how you got drunk and told everyone that you wanted to get
me pregnant using a dildo

DAVID
I did not!

JESSICA
I have it on video

DAVID
Well…

JESSICA
It's on YouTube

DAVID
How many hits?

JESSICA

How crazy are you?

DAVID
How cute am I?

JESSICA
You were very, very cute and I loved you.

DAVID
And at what point did you stop?

(PAUSE)

JESSICA
What?

DAVID
At what point did you stop?

JESSICA
At what point did I stop what?

DAVID
Thinking I was cute and falling for me?

JESSICA
You asshole

DAVID
What?

JESSICA
You are a fucking asshole!!

DAVID
What?

JESSICA
I never stopped loving you!

DAVID
Yea right

JESSICA
Is this what this is all about? What makes you think I changed my mind
about you at all?

DAVID
What about that guy you were all cozy with?

JESSICA
What guy?

DAVID
The guy at the bar

JESSICA
The guy at the bar?

DAVID
Yes, 3 years into our relationship, we go to a bar and you were all over
that guy at the bar

JESSICA
The guy at the bar?

DAVID
The guy at the bar

JESSICA
I was all over the guy at the bar...okay...that was my NEPHEW, you
mental midget!

DAVID
That was what?

JESSICA
That was my nephew, he just turned 21 you fuck tard! I hadn't seen him
in years so of course, I was all over him, is that why you gave me the
silent treatment all night?

DAVID
No...

JESSICA
You fucking horse's dick!!

DAVID
How the fuck was I supposed to know that?

JESSICA
He was at my sister's wedding, the one we went to in our second year,
dickweed

DAVID
Wait really? He had short hair

JESSICA

No shit, Sherlock, his parents made him cut it off because he got into
ROTC?!

DAVID
It does make sense

JESSICA
Yea...and what about you and the blonde?

DAVID
The blonde?

JESSICA
The blonde!

DAVID
The blonde was after the guy at the bar, I wanted revenge.

JESSICA
You wanted revenge?

DAVID
Yes, I wanted revenge

JESSICA
How fucking petty are you?

DAVID
The best in Boston, baby.

JESSICA
This is serious

DAVID
Yes

JESSICA
What alternative dimension were you living in. So that's why a year
after that you stayed around? That makes no sense. Why didn't we
break up?

DAVID
I spent the rest of the time trying to figure out if you still loved me.

JESSICA
For a year?! Couldn't the times when I said I loved you give you a
fucking hint about where I was?!

DAVID
I'm not a mind reader.

JESSICA
Who are you?!

DAVID
Love did something to me

JESSICA
Made you stupid?!

DAVID
Hey, I've called you a lot of things and you've called me a lot of things,
but don't you dare ever call me stupid. That's just hurtful. I was so
afraid you'd wake up one day and realize I was crazy, and, on that day,
you would decide that you had enough, and you'd pack up and leave. I
was delaying the inevitable.

JESSICA

David that was every day for a year!! I always knew you were crazy, but I loved you for it. I looked at you every day and thanked God I had you. I spend most of the time wondering why you were with me. Did I ever stop loving you? Never, not once, not even the days you were a douche.

DAVID

I was never a douche.

JESSICA

Oh, Valentine's Day, Valentine's day you could be a real douche.

DAVID

Just because I locked myself in a room and…

JESSICA

You wouldn't even come out to pee! You went all Howard Hughes and pissed in mason jars which by the way, the cat drank out of.

DAVID

That sounds like a personal problem.

JESSICA

No, you know what a personal problem was, while you were away in the room with tissue boxes on your feet, I had to go out and treat myself and then clean up after the fucking cat?!

DAVID

Okay I could be a little bit of a douche

JESSICA

A little bit?

DAVID
Okay a lot, Jesus. I can only imagine it getting worst if we got married

JESSICA
What?

DAVID
I said I can only imagine it getting worst if I had asked you to marry me.

JESSICA
Did you?

DAVID
What?

JESSICA
Did you want to marry me?

DAVID
Of course, …

JESSICA
Why didn't you want to ask me?

DAVID
I did…I just didn't think you'd say yes. That's why I never asked and then…well big things became small things and small things became big things.

JESSICA
You wanted to ask me to marry you?

DAVID
Yes

(PAUSE)

JESSICA
Wow...I didn't know that.

DAVID
Yea...

JESSICA
So why did we break up?

DAVID
You hated me

JESSICA
What?

DAVID
You hated me

JESSICA
I didn't hate you

DAVID
You left.

JESSICA
You were supposed to stop me?!

DAVID
I couldn't...

JESSICA
Why?

DAVID
Because after spending four years of you calling me every name in the
book, I realized that maybe you were right.

JESSICA
What?

DAVID
When you called me every name in the...?

JESSICA
When did I do that?

DAVID
All the time!

JESSICA
I never called you anything but silly, stupid!

DAVID
Yes, you have.

JESSICA
Name one time I called you anything worse than stupid.

DAVID
You want me to name one time you called me a bad name?

JESSICA
Yes!

DAVID
Okay…let me take a moment and think about that to see if I can remember…. You've been doing it this whole time!

JESSICA
What?

DAVID
You have been calling me every name in the book ever since we got stuck in this hotel room!

JESSICA
Oh…I didn't realize.

DAVID
You have…

JESSICA
Really?

DAVID
Yes!

JESSICA
Oh my…

DAVID
So, I figured you were right.

JESSICA
What do you mean?

DAVID
I have a big ego, and with that you sometimes don't see who you really are. I'm a douche. I'm a dick. I am a dick weed in the rocks on turd mountain. I am a no-good son of a bitch. You called me that a lot and after hearing it all the time, I realized you were right.

JESSICA
You did?

DAVID
Yea so I let you go, and I sold the apartment and moved away because I felt like I couldn't have failed any worse than when I failed with you. To say there, would have just been a constant reminder of what I fucked up.

JESSICA
Really? That's why when I went back you weren't there?

DAVID
You went back?

JESSICA
Yea three days later, I wanted to talk it out and fix it.

DAVID
Two days after you left, I left.

JESSICA
Wow. I didn't know that.

DAVID
Yea so that's my secret.

JESSICA
I didn't know I called you all those names all the time.

DAVID
That's not a secret.

JESSICA
I'm sorry, David. I'm sorry I never realized how mean that could be. I
was being snarky and playful.

DAVID
It was, some of the time, but other times, like tonight, it was hurtful.

JESSICA
I am sorry, David.

DAVID
Thank you. I even got the ring.

(PAUSE)

JESSICA
What?

DAVID
I had bought a ring.

David pulls out a ring and shows it to Jessica.

JESSICA

You had it on you this whole time?!

DAVID
Well I don't have a safety deposit box!

JESSICA
Wow...well if you were to ask a woman to marry you, that's the ring to get her.

Jessica continues to look at the ring.

JESSICA
You wanna know something?

DAVID
What?

JESSICA
I would have said yes if you asked me to marry you.

DAVID
What?

JESSICA
I would have said yes

DAVID
You would have?

JESSICA
David, I loved you. My mind was filled with nothing but David! You were all I could think about. Every day I got through my work so quickly because I wanted to get home and snuggle up next to you. I wanted to

stand on an altar and vow myself to you. I wanted to set up a house with you and live the rest of my life as your wife. I wanted to bear your child and name him something we chose together. I wanted to see that child grow up with both of us there to be a parent to the child. I wanted to see him go from diapers to grad school in the blink of an eye. I wanted to then grow old with you. I wanted to hold you close for the rest of my life knowing that when I said yes to you wanting to marry me that I couldn't have made a better decision. That's my secret

DAVID
Wow.

JESSICA
David, I really miss you

DAVID
You do?

JESSICA
Before tonight, yes, I think about you often

DAVID
Well I miss you too and I thought about you a lot as well.

JESSICA
David?

DAVID
Yes?

JESSICA
Do you still love me?

(PAUSE)

DAVID
I do, I always will, you were my first love.

JESSICA
I will always love you too, for better or for worst for rich or poorer for sickness or in health to death do us part. You were my first as well.

DAVID
Wow

(PAUSE)

DAVID
It would have been a nice wedding

JESSICA
Damn Skippy and I would have looked hot in a wedding dress.

DAVID
Yea you would have

JESSICA
Damn hot

DAVID
I can only imagine how many dresses it would have taken for you to choose the right one.

JESSICA
Oh, shut up! You would have loved every minute.

DAVID
I would have loved to argue about the type of invitations, not only the
type but the paper that the invitations and the lettering on the
invitations and then the envelopes of the invitations.

JESSICA
Oh, you would have complained the whole time about random shit, but
you would have liked the food.

DAVID
Oh, hell yeah. I would have gone all Jurassic Park on that and spared no
expense.

JESSICA
Would you have written your own vows?

DAVID
I would have written both of ours.

JESSICA
What makes you think I would have said the same things.

DAVID
Okay I would have written them and then you would have re-written
them.

JESSICA
Very true.

DAVID
Your mother would have cried.

JESSICA

Yes, she would have.

DAVID
I can hear her crying now, "Don't do it! Run Away!"

JESSICA
Yea you are probably right but she didn't know you like I did.

DAVID
Well she is the one who had the voodoo doll.

They both start laughing.

JESSICA
Storm's letting up

DAVID
Well let's go down to the lobby and check out the damage.

JESSICA
Oh…you don't want to stay up here.

DAVID
No, there might be some interesting damage down there.

Jessica looks out the window.

JESSICA
It's all clean up now. No more debris

DAVID
Well maybe there's a transformer or something…

JESSICA
You going to save my life again?

DAVID
Hmmm...

JESSICA
Don't answer that

DAVID
I mean we can head out now.

JESSICA
Yea...

DAVID
So, Jess, good to see you... (starts to leave)

JESSICA
David...you know I don't have to be back home until Monday...we could
get the room for another night or so.

DAVID
Really? You aren't sick of me?

JESSICA
I didn't say that.

DAVID
Oh...

JESSICA
Maybe we can start again where we left off.

DAVID
You're not done with me?

JESSICA
I don't think so.

DAVID
Wow.

JESSICA
I mean if you want to leave that's fine, I just thought...

DAVID
I didn't say that...I was just looking for the right...umm...

JESSICA
Answer?

DAVID
Moment.

Jessica extends her hand to David as David takes her hand and they move close to each other. Jessica puts her arms around David as David puts his arms around her waist.

JESSICA
Can I see that ring again?

DAVID
Sure...

David pulls it out and gets on his knee and looks up to her and hands it to her. She nods her head in the affirmative and he gets up and wraps his arms around her. They look at each other as they lean in to...

The lights go down quickly and then come up to David waking up in a bed.

DAVID
Oh, my budda!

David's wife, who you could not see before and is not Jessica, wakes up with him.

DAVID'S WIFE
Honey, are you okay?

Lights come up to another bed with Jessica waking up in it.

JESSICA
Oh, my goodness, where am I?

Jessica's husband, again someone who you could not see before and is not David, wake up next to her

JESSICA'S HUSBAND
Babe, you need some water?

DAVID
Yea, yea I'm okay

JESSICA
No, no, I'm good

Both
Just a dream

DAVID'S WIFE
A good one?

JESSICA's HUSBAND
What was it about?

BOTH
Someone I knew a long time ago...

DAVID
Can I get some water?

JESSICA
Actually, some water would be nice.

The spouses leave. The lights go down with a single spotlight on Jessica and David. They each reach down to the nightstand and pick up their phones. They begin to dial but stop themselves. They look towards the direction of each other.

JESSICA
Goodbye...

DAVID
Goodbye...

as the lights go down.

END OF ACT TWO

THE END

ACKNOWLEDGEMENTS
First of all, I have to thank my wife, Megan who not only edited this collection and helped me put this whole thing together but has had the enthusiasm and patience to support and help me in my career as a playwright and a director. To say that she has sacrificed much is the world's biggest understatement. I don't think that when we got married that she would have imagined such a life like ours. Sometimes unpredictable and sometimes difficult, mostly because of my doing, but the fact that she has continued to support me and never once discouraged me or my career, she's a saint. I wouldn't be anywhere close to where I am and have the confidence I have if it wasn't for her.

I need to also thank my mother. She introduced me to theater at such a young age and got me hooked immediately. She does have a realistic approach to life and wanted to make sure I had a good job and could support my family but she has been to every show I have directed and most of the shows that I actually wrote. She was my first and original cheerleader and when she says to me that she is very proud of me then

I don't think there's an award out there that I could get that would make me feel more accomplished than that.

I do want to thank my father. He was never really big on the whole me being a part of theater and creative worlds when I could be making a living and supporting my family in more commercial and financially satisfying ways but I do hope he realizes how much material he has given me over the years and I honestly hope that I made him proud.

I want to finish by saying thank you to my grandmother, Mary Pomphrey. Before she passed years ago, she told me to continue to follow my passion and never give up and reach for the stars. Her words have guided me through some tough times in this life and career but ultimately I really hope I made her proud.

I want to thank Damien and Anetta for putting their relationship at risk by playing a feuding couple in this weird circumstance. I will say they are amazing and they also helped very much re-shape this play. They created these characters and developed them and brought them to life and I will always be grateful to them for that.

I also want to thank some of the women and men who inspired these characters and their affect on my life. As I said, I haven't been in that many relationships but this was definitely inspired by most of them and I am grateful to them.

ABOUT THE AUTHOR

Matthew Garlin Author

His acting credits include Quannapowitt Players: Suburban Holidays 3, 4, 5 & 6 and A Midsummer Night's Dream, Theatre to Go: Arsenic and Old Lace and Twelfth Night, New England School of Performing Arts: The Breakfast Club and The Bard Brigade: The Tempest, The Merchant of Venice, and Macbeth, Revolutionary Theatre: Shakespeare Academy, Still Small theatre's repertory company for How I Met Our Father and The Diary of Perpetua. His directing credits include Enchanted April for Theatre to Go Inc., Almost Maine and It's a Wonderful Life for Theater Company of Saugus, Godspell for Sherwood Entertainment, Side by Side by Sondheim for Colonial Chorus Players, Twelfth Night for The Bard Brigade, and a short film Project Invisible. His playwright credits include: Online Dating (one act play) and Curtain Call (Full length play) at Acting Out Company in Lawrence, How Do You Know (one act play) at River's Edge Arts Alliance, Woods (full length play) at Theater@First, and A Christmas Gift (one act play) at Theater

company of Saugus. His composer credits include: Almost Maine for Theater Company
of Saugus, Macbeth, and Much Ado About Nothing for The Bard Brigade Enchanted
April for Theatre to Go.